A CREATIVE KEEPSAKE

paige tate & CO.
www.paigetate.com

Published in 2017 by
Paige Tate & Co.
An Imprint of PCG Publishing LLC
3610 Avenue B
San Antonio, TX 78209
email: reagan@paigetate.com
www.paigetate.com

All rights reserved. No part of this publication may be reproduced or transmitted in any form or by any means, electronic or mechanical, including photocopy, recording or any information storage and retrieval system, without permission in writing from the publisher.

ISBN: 978-1944515386
Printed in China

Scripture quotations are from the following:

Scriptures taken from the Holy Bible, New International Version®, NIV®. Copyright © 1973, 1978,1984, 2011 by Biblica, Inc.TM Used by permission of Zondervan. All rights reserved worldwide. www.zondervan.com The "NIV" and "New International Version" are trademarks registered in the United States Patent and Trademark Office by Biblica, Inc.TM

Scripture quotations marked ESV are from the ESV® Bible (The Holy Bible, English Standard Version®), copyright © 2001 by Crossway, a publishing ministry of Good News Publishers. Used by permission. All rights reserved.

FIND ALL OF OUR PRODUCTS AT

www.paigetate.com

AND FOLLOW US ON INSTAGRAM AT

@PAIGETATEANDCO

ABOUT THE AUTHOR

Amanda Arneill

Amanda is a hand-lettering artist and instructor who has inspired many all over the world to combine their love of Jesus with their love of lettering and delve deeper into the scripture. As the mom of two, a wife, and the owner of a successful business, Amanda knows the importance of slowing down in this busy world to take time with God.

Addicted to all things lettering, irrationally excited by new pens and determined to spend as many working days as possible in sweatpants, Amanda has built a dedicated and ever-growing following of lettering lovers.

You can find out more about her and her work at
amandaarneill.com

why church journaling

My Christian story is not unlike many others out there. I've gone to church for my entire life and sat through many sermons, some good and some not so good. Regardless of who was preaching, I've always wanted to learn as much about God as possible while I was in church, but that wasn't always happening.

At some point, without fail, my mind would wander. I would start thinking about what to make for dinner, my plans for the next week or just where the woman two rows ahead of me got that fabulous dress. My mind would be anywhere but on the message that God wanted me to hear to take me through the upcoming week.

I was sick of the struggle, so I set out to find some way to change it. I had begun to do calligraphy and hand lettering, and I thought it might be a great idea to letter out some of the things discussed during church. I would take my journal, start to jot down a few sermon quotes with pencil and then letter them out. It led to some nice lettering, but while I was lettering, again, my mind would wander. I didn't need to be engaged in the sermon to do the lettering that I was doing. I needed something more.

So I posed myself with a challenge. Rather than writing down a few of the things that were said, I would try to letter the whole sermon, not word for word, but by capturing all of the main points and supporting statements. I would not stop writing down what was said until the sermon was done. I had to accept that this would mean that I might not be doing my most beautiful lettering, but that wasn't the point of my Church Journal.

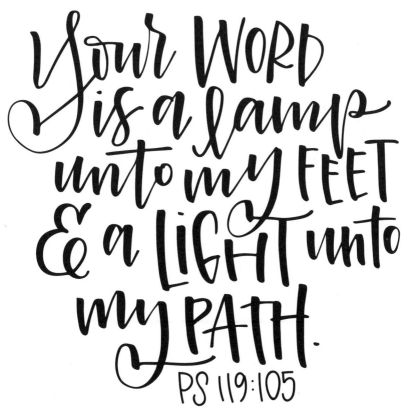

Your WORD is a lamp unto my FEET & a LIGHT unto my PATH. PS 119:105

My first week of church journaling was stressful because of the expectations that I had for myself and my lettering was far from perfect! The letters were messy,

the spacing wasn't consistent, and my doodles weren't professional… but there was so much more there. Church journaling was life changing!

I was attentive every minute of the sermon, I could remember what was said and, though the individual letters weren't my best, together they looked beautiful.

That was the beginning of my church journaling story.

As a lettering artist, I have had the privilege of working with companies of all sizes. I've helped some amazing charities raise money for their cause, and I've donated a big portion of the money I've earned with lettering to causes that I'm really passionate about. However nothing in my life has made as large a difference in my journey with God as church journaling.

Lettering in church reignited my desire to hear God's word. It stopped my mind from wandering and brought me closer to God and living in His word because I was *completely mentally present* for it. Every Sunday, I look forward to the moment that I get to pull out my Church

Journal and learn more about the amazing message that God has in store for me.

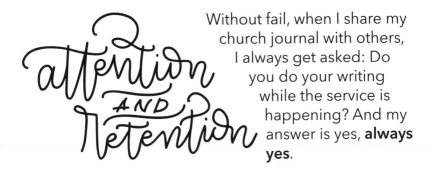

Without fail, when I share my church journal with others, I always get asked: Do you do your writing while the service is happening? And my answer is yes, **always yes**.

My goal with church journaling is to engage in attentive listening to God's word, and the way I do that is by writing the service as it happens. That means, yep, I write as I go.

There are a few things that I've had to release to make that happen such as the layout, composition, letter forms and spacing (and looking at that list, I realize those are the primary steps of lettering). But church journaling isn't about lettering for others. It is lettering for yourself to grow your relationship with God.

I would encourage you to use this book to draw near to God, rather than to achieve perfection. Release yourself from creating something for others and instead, create something perfect for you. Remember, God wants you to be present, not perfect.

lettering VERSUS note taking

We write notes to ourselves all day long in the form of grocery lists, to-do reminders, and scribbles here and there. But lettering is so much more intentional and it allows you to be fully engaged. What more could you want when you're sitting in church listening to God's word?!

Lettering uses not only the language parts of your brain but also the artistic parts as well. Getting more of your brain involved allows you to better focus on the sermon and retain the message even days after the service.

Putting your church lettering into this one book will allow you to create a keepsake of weekly services and also your faith journey. It is something that you will be proud to look at over and over again. I love flipping through my book and revisiting truths about God from weeks and months past.

Remember that church journaling is intended to be something that happens during the service as it unfolds. From the moment the service begins until its end, I can be found with my church journal in my lap, pen moving the whole time.

I try to *include*

- mentioned verses
- the main points of the service as it happens
- statements that stand out to me
- important points
- anything that I want to review again later

I *DON'T include*

- every word said
- anything that is being repeated
- main points that I may have missed because I was still lettering something else (and I don't stress because I know that another main point will be coming soon)

Sometimes I also *include*

- song lyrics
- related thoughts
- doodles to illustrate an idea or topic

my lettering strategy

Now you know what I focus on and what things I let go, but there's also the lettering to take into account. I typically try to use simple lettering styles. Every so often you'll see a more elaborate style, background sketches or shadow effect added to my letters but, since those take longer, they don't happen as often.

Here's my secret.... I do those more time consuming design elements during "slow" portions of the sermon such as when the pastor is telling a story to illustrate a point or making announcements that I don't need to write down. That's when I look over my page and add in the special touches.

Some days I am able to add more than others and that's totally okay.

Here's a basic idea of what I add:

- *2 - 3 shadowed blocks*
- *1 - 2 doodles*
- *1 - 2 script areas*
- *1 - 2 arrows*
- *1 - 2 other visual embellishments*

I try to spread these around the page to keep them visually balanced, but all of these added elements are the perfect way to fill up any spaces that may have shown up on your page in between your lettering areas.

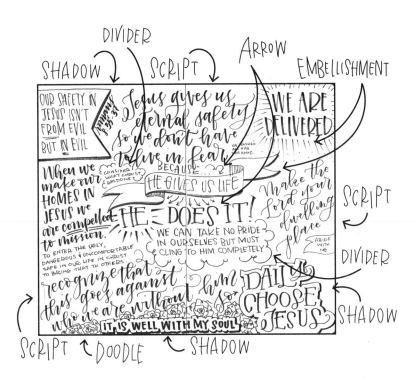

The labels surrounding the journaling page read:

SHADOW — DIVIDER — SCRIPT — ARROW — EMBELLISHMENT

SCRIPT — DIVIDER — SHADOW

SCRIPT — DOODLE — SHADOW

Text within the journal page:

OUR SAFETY IN JESUS ISN'T FROM EVIL BUT IN EVIL

Jeremiah 8:15-34

Jesus gives us eternal safety so we don't have to live in fear

WE ARE DELIVERED

He washed our sins away.

When we make our HOMES IN JESUS we are compelled to mission.

CONSIDER WHAT CHRIST HAS DONE

BECAUSE

HE GIVES US LIFE

HE = DOES IT!

WE CAN TAKE NO PRIDE IN OURSELVES BUT MUST CLING TO HIM COMPLETELY

make the Lord your dwelling place

ABIDE WITH ME

To enter the ugly, dangerous & uncomfortable safe in our life in Christ to bring that to others.

recognize that this goes against who we are without him so

DAILY CHOOSE JESUS

IT IS WELL WITH MY SOUL

Writing IN YOUR Journal

The most important thing you can do to make your church journaling easy to read is to use a different lettering style for any notes written beside one another (either that or use some sort of drawn divider).

Don't worry! This doesn't mean that you have to create a unique lettering style for each idea, and you can't ever repeat it. That would be impossible!

I like to pick a few lettering styles and just alternate through them. By rotating styles, your notes will be much easier to read and will have so much more visual interest.

If you need help with some lettering inspiration, make sure that you check out pages 29 - 30 for lots of sample alphabets!

What makes church lettering look so amazing is that it results in a solid page of lettering notes, but holes in the design weaken that effect. If you're struggling to figure out what to use in a hole, take a peek at page 28 where you will find many different ideas to get your creative juices flowing.

When I letter at home, my workspace is a mess. I have lots of space to spread out and use many different pens and instruments. At church, I keep it to the basics only.

Of course, I have my church journal, but I also bring one pencil, an eraser, and two pens. When I'm lettering during the sermon, I only use one of my pens, but always have a backup in case I drop the first one, it rolls away, or one of my kids snatches it and runs.

Because I do all of my church journaling on my lap, I like to use a more rigid pen so that I can include lots of details. I choose to use a Tombow Fudenosuke hard nib brush pen so that the thickness of the line varies with the pressure that I put on the pen. Using a pen like this is a great way to have lots of variety but only have to carry along a single tool.

I will warn you that brush pens can take some getting used to, and if you aren't comfortable with them, a simple 0.3mm or 0.5mm micron pen is a great alternative for church journaling.

how to use
your church journal

This journal is set out to give you the framework to make church journaling simple for you.

Each week is separated into a few key pages. There is the main starter page with a place for the week's scripture, prayer requests and a place for quick note taking.

The next spread is two pages that are blank for your church journaling. This is where the magic will happen. These pages are what you will fill with the message from the week while it is happening. There are no lines or guides or structure to these pages as your church experience is different week to week.

Don't worry about filling in the spread in a specific direction or style. Move around the page and write down your notes and thoughts as they happen. You can always link points with arrows or doodles if you need to provide some flow to your notes.

You can see a video example of my church journal page creation at www.churchjournaling.com to give you a guide, and hopefully, the freedom to write as you go without limitations or constraints.

For church journaling, I use a variety of lettering styles to write my notes, rather than my actual handwriting, which I consider to be messy, and not something that I would see as keepsake worthy.

I also use doodles and line dividers as well as changes in lettering style to create visual differences between distinct points of the sermon.

Before we even start to talk about lettering or embellishments or anything else like that, we need to establish a few basic guidelines for church journaling.

key points

1. Capture the main points of the sermon, not every word.

2. Don't worry about making it pretty. It is the word of God, so there's nothing you can do to make it any more perfect than it already is.

3. Forgive yourself for spelling mistakes (this is a big one for me!).

4. Use doodles or simple drawings to help make the sermon come alive. You don't need to be an artist to draw!

5. Be free and kind to yourself! Try new things and don't worry about perfection.

Alphabets

Alphabet styles can be super simple or incredibly complex.

Because a sermon moves quickly, focus on using lettering styles that are quick and easy to write. I have four main styles that I rotate through, and then I go back and embellish my lettering with shadows, outlines, and doodles during breaks in the sermon.

The basic alphabet that I build off of is an engineer style capital.

ABCDEFGHI
JKLMNOPQ
RSTUVWXYZ

However, if this style were all that I used, it would be hard to create distinct visual areas of text.

By changing the size, width, height, slant, thickness and shadow of a simple lettering style, we can alter this basic letter form to make it look totally different.

SIZE

The simplest way to add distinction to certain words is by changing the writing size.

I use larger letters for main ideas during the service and smaller letters for side thoughts that I have, things the pastor mentions in passing or song lyrics that speak to me.

When used side by side, varying the size creates obvious distinctions between parts of your lettering.

SLANT

Your printed alphabet can also change by angling the letters.

The main thing to keep in mind with an angled alphabet is to be consistent with your angle. I usually wing it, but you can sketch simple guidelines in pencil if necessary to guide your angled letters.

ABCDEFGHIJKLMNOPQRSTUVWXYZ

THICKNESS

Just like bolding your text in an email or document, creating a bold letter gives it more weight and importance. It is a great way to make some of your lettering stand apart.

There are easy and quick ways to bold your letters.

One would be to use a thicker pen. This will automatically create a thicker line.

But, if you're anything like me, having more than one pen out at a time is a recipe for a loud, embarrassing, pen-dropping disaster. Instead of using a second pen, I simply draw another line beside each of the lines in my piece and then I connect them and fill them in.

OUTLINE AND Shadow

During pauses and breaks in the service, you can pick main words, phrases or ideas that you want to add a little something special to and create an outline or shadow effect.

STEP 1

Draw your letters as you want them.

STEP 2

Draw an outline around the lettering as a whole. Try to keep the outline at a consistent distance from the letters.

STEP 3

On one side of the outline, and along the bottom, create a thicker line to mimic the effect of a shadow. Practice creating shadows on either side to find which one you prefer.

 Using a script alphabet is a gorgeous and dramatic way to add another lettering style to your church journaling.

You can use a variation of your handwriting or refer to the alphabet below for a more stylized alphabet.

When I use script, I typically don't use capitals except in names. That is just part of my personal preference and is the complete opposite of my printed alphabet.

A script alphabet can be altered with the same changes as the printed alphabet. You can make the script larger or smaller, give it a slant, or add thicker areas to your lettering. I'll be going into creating thick areas on letters in the next few sections on faux-ligraphy and brush lettering.

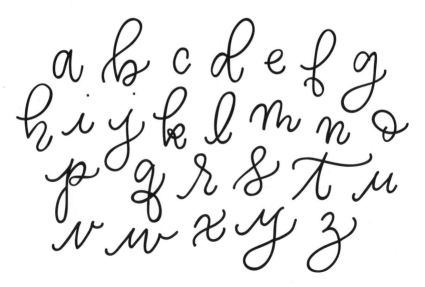

PSALM 78:70-72 WORK | CALLING | READ THE SCRIPTURES WITH God AT THE CENTRE

NOT JUST WORK BUT WORK IN FAITH

COMPETENCY

how out does our faith in Jesus reflect in our vocation & work

CHARACTER

THIS PSALM COVERS CENTURIES SO, LIKE THE ENTIRE BIBLE, IT IS ACTUALLY A STORY OF GOD, NOT MAN.

reminds us of what God has done & reveal his glory.

HONOUR GOD'S CALLING YOUR WORK

OUR CALLING NEEDS TO BE REMEMBERED IN THE LIGHT OF GOD'S GRAND NARRATIVE

TAKE YOUR IMPORTANCE DOWN A NOTCH!

HIM NOT ME

GOD'S STORY IMPACTS OUR CALLING

FOLD OUR STORY INTO THE GREATER STORY OF GOD.

USE YOUR CALLING TO BUILD UP THE BODY OF CHRIST.

DO WHAT YOU DO WELL AS UNTO GOD

DAVID WAS A SHEPHERD THAT GOD MADE A KING

What does SUCCESS look like in the light of this?

FOLLOW YOUR GIFTS, AFFINITIES & WHAT GIVES YOU JOY &

do it unto the Lord

"INTEGRITY OF HEART" DAVID WAS A MESS BUT UNDERSTOOD HIS PLACE BEFORE GOD.

GOD IS GOD

calligraphy

You are totally able to make gorgeous lettering with a regular Micron or other bullet nib pen, but if you want to add lots of variety to your lettering, the basics of brush lettering (a form of calligraphy) are where it's at! There are specific pens, appropriately named "brush pens," that should be used for brush lettering. These pens have a flexible felt or nylon tip and, as you apply pressure to your pen, the thickness of your line increases.

I will warn you that brush pens do take practice to use, so don't be discouraged if it doesn't come naturally right away. That's why I'll also teach you a bit of faux-ligraphy here so that you can get the beauty of brush lettering without the trickiness of using a brush pen.

finding your downstrokes

All lettering is made up of a few components: downstrokes, upstrokes and cross strokes. When you write a letter, your pen moves different ways across the page.

When your pen moves down the page toward you, you're creating a "downstroke."

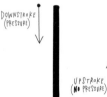

When your pen moves away from you, that's an "upstroke."

And any time that your pen moves horizontally across the page (for example, to cross a t or curve under a y), that is a "cross stroke."

The key of fauxligraphy and brush lettering is to zone in on those downstrokes and make all of them thicker.

To find downstrokes, you can either use the fauxligraphy alphabet outline as a cheat sheet or you can pay attention to the movement of your hand.

faux-ligraphy

Start off with writing out your letter. Keep in mind that many letters are made of multiple lines so it might help you to visualize them as if they were broken apart from one another.

After you write the components, look at the way that your pen moved across the page.

I like to "ghost trace" the letters (rewrite it without touching the page) and everytime that my pen moves downwards, I draw that line in, slightly to the side of the line already on the page. This leaves me with a letter that has some areas of a single line (on the upstrokes and cross strokes) and areas of double lines (the downstrokes).

Once you have your double lines drawn in, color in that space between the lines to give the appearance of naturally drawn, thicker downstrokes.

a b c d e f g
h i j k l m n
o p q r s t u
v w x y z

Jesus gives EVIDENCE for faith
THE DISCIPLES SAW THE RESURRECTED JESUS

OUR EVIDENCE IS THE WORD OF THE LORD AND EYE WITNESSES

remove your

BECAUSE FOR THE FIRST TIME THEY HAD TO WALK IN FAITH.

THE BIBLE

worship move past FEAR DOUBT

JOHN 20 RESURRECTION AND MISSION

THROW IT OFF

can be HARD to see past

JESUS when we are FOCUSED on FEAR

WILL HIM JESUS

THE RISEN KING with SCARS

Peace be with you now go

FEAR OF THE WORLD CAN'T MOVE BEYOND WHAT'S IN FRONT OF US ON

as the focus

JESUS needs to be our

MOVE FROM AN ENCOUNTER TO A MISSION

JOHN 5:30 JOHN 6:29
JOHN 5:36 JOHN 17:18
JOHN 6:38

CENTRE

obedience to GOD gives authority IN MISSION!

earth to MOVE PAST FEAR

24

Brush lettering takes the same principles as fauxligraphy except that, instead of drawing the double line to achieve your thick downstroke, you use the flexible nib of the pen to create a thicker line.

During brush lettering, you only write the word once (no "ghost tracing" here!). As you create your letters, any time that you create a downstroke (when your pen moves down the page), you want to put pressure on the pen to cause the nib to flex and create a thicker line. On upstrokes (when your pen moves up the page), don't put any pressure on the pen. Only use the tip of the pen as if you are "tickling" the page. When you remove the pressure off of the pen, the nib flexes back to revert to the thinner line.

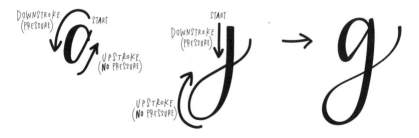

With practice, this style of writing becomes quick and easy, but it is best learned in a live workshop or thorough an online course (like my beginner level course at www.amandaarneill.com/startlettering).

creating lettering blocks

When you're writing in your church journal, don't worry about writing from left to right in an orderly fashion. Instead, think about writing in blocks, creating squares and rectangles of words. Visually, this will help to make your work easier to read and keep different ideas separate from one another. Each block of text should be written in a different style and size to help create distinct idea blocks.

One of the ways I make sure my page doesn't just look like a mess of letters is to ensure that none of the journal notes that sit next to one another use the same style.

Praise the Lord

Psalm 148

List of various things that were created to praise the Lord.

100 billion galaxies × 100 billion stars & God knows each of them by name

HE COMMANDED & THEY WERE CREATED

PRAISE AT BOTH THE BEGINNING AND THE END

everything was made by him to pour forth Praise

Nothing in creation is an accident!!

Genesis 3 - the PERFECT praise of MAN was removed by SIN (PART OF GOD'S PERFECT CREATION)

WE WERE MADE TO PRAISE HIM

we are given grace

DAILY YOUR LIFE NEEDS TO SING PRAISE TO THE LORD... make your day-to-day praise the Lord

PRAISE HIM BECAUSE YOU LOVE HIM.

...EVERY DAY IN EVERY WAY TO HIM... ESPECIALLY WHEN YOU ARE ALONE!

WE HAVE BEEN redeemed BY JESUS' BLOOD

He is greater than our praise COULD EVER EXPRESS. No Limit!

Having some sections of writing that are lighter, just regular print using the tip of your pen, helps to create areas of visual lightness throughout your page. This makes the entire page easier to read and it is also a great way to be able to write a chunk of your notes in a quicker, more traditional lettering style!

You can also use line dividers, squares and ribbons to separate one thought from another.

I often use doodles as visual dividers between sections or in the middle of a page.

Now, I'm most definitely not a pro at drawing, but the doodles look great within the page and help to illustrate the ideas of the sermon. So even if you think that you can't draw, start with something simple and, I promise, it will only add to the beauty of your journaled page.

doodles AND dividers

more alphabets

ABCDEF
GHIJKL
MNOPRST
UVWXYZ

ABCDEFGH
IJKLMNOPQ
RSTUVWXYZ

One final note

Because church journaling means that you have to write quickly, when you first start out, just focus on lettering the big ideas. As you get faster and lettering becomes easier for you, start to use more styles in your writing. As that gets simple for you, start to add in embellishments and doodles to fill in your page. Over time, you'll be able to do more each week!

Whatever styles you choose to use, I want to remind you that God doesn't care what your handwriting looks like, He just wants you to be with Him! So use your church journal to be present, engaged and in relationship with the Lord.

XO,
amanda

Learn more at churchjournaling.com

Today's verse

DATE

quick notes _____
_____
_____
_____
_____

prayer items

Today's verse

DATE

quick notes

_____
_____
_____
_____
_____

prayer items

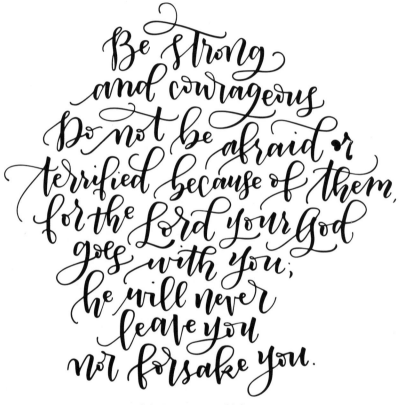

Be strong and courageous. Do not be afraid or terrified because of them, for the Lord your God goes with you; he will never leave you nor forsake you.

DEUTERONOMY 31:6

Today's verse

DATE

quick notes

_____
_____
_____
_____
_____

prayer items

Today's verse

DATE

quick notes

_____

_____

_____

_____

_____

prayer items

For freedom Christ has set us free GALATIANS 5:1

Today's verse

DATE

quick notes

_____
_____
_____
_____
_____

prayer items

You will Keep in PERFECT peace those whose MINDS are STEADFAST, because they TRUST in YOU

ISAIAH 26:3

Today's verse

DATE

quick notes

_____
_____
_____
_____
_____

prayer items

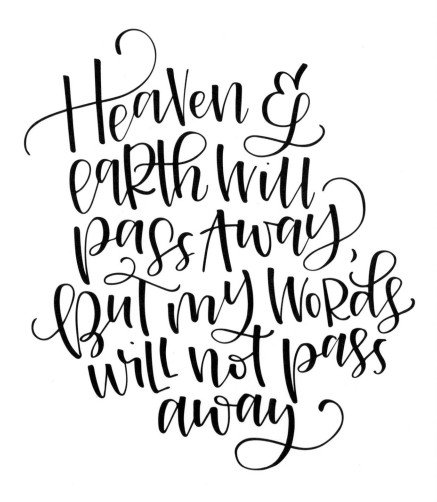

Today's verse

DATE

quick notes

_____
_____
_____
_____
_____

prayer items

The Lord replied, "My presence will go with you and I will give you rest."

EXODUS 33:14

Today's verse

DATE

quick notes

_____

_____

_____

_____

_____

prayer items

Today's verse

DATE

quick notes

_____

_____

_____

_____

_____

prayer items

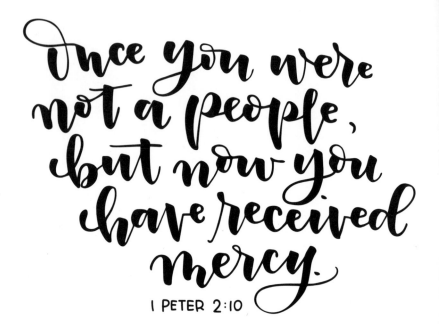

Once you were not a people, but now you have received mercy.

1 PETER 2:10

Today's verse

DATE

quick notes

_____
_____
_____
_____
_____

prayer items

Today's verse

DATE

quick notes _____
_____
_____
_____
_____

prayer
items

trust in the Lord
with all your heart and
lean not on your own
understanding;
in all your ways
submit to him
and he will make
your paths straight.

PROVERBS 3:5-6

Today's verse

DATE

quick notes _____
_____
_____
_____
_____

prayer items

And you will know the truth and the truth will set you FREE

JOHN 8:32

Today's verse

DATE

quick notes

_____
_____
_____
_____
_____

prayer items

Today's verse

DATE

quick notes _____
_____
_____
_____
_____

prayer
items

GOD is our REFUGE and STRENGTH, an everpresent HELP in TROUBLE

PSALM 46:1

Today's verse

DATE

quick notes

_____

_____

_____

_____

prayer items

Turn from evil & do good; Seek peace and pursue it.

Today's verse

DATE

quick notes

_____
_____
_____
_____
_____

prayer items

Today's verse

DATE

quick notes

_____
_____
_____
_____
_____

prayer items

Today's verse

DATE

quick notes _____

_____

_____

_____

_____

prayer items

Today's verse

DATE

quick notes

_____
_____
_____
_____
_____

prayer items

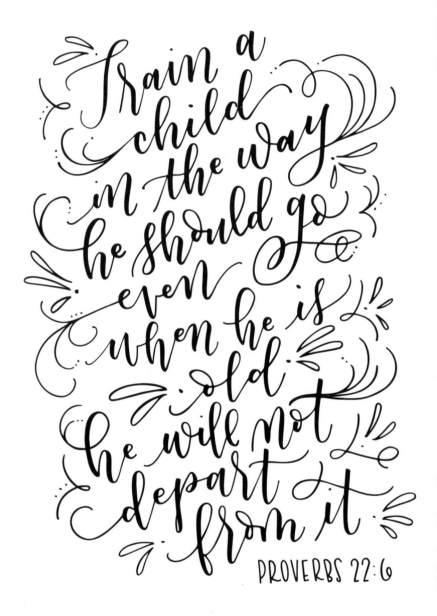

Train a child in the way he should go even when he is old he will not depart from it

PROVERBS 22:6

Today's verse

DATE

quick notes

_____

_____

_____

_____

_____

prayer items

disciple

Today's verse

DATE

quick notes

_____
_____
_____
_____
_____

prayer items

Today's verse

DATE

quick notes

_____
_____
_____
_____
_____

prayer items

the
LOVE
of God is
from Genesis
to Revelation

Today's verse

DATE

quick notes

_____
_____
_____
_____
_____

prayer items

Today's verse

DATE

quick notes

_____
_____
_____
_____
_____

prayer items

Come Thou Fount
of every blessing
Tune my heart to
sing Thy grace.
Streams of mercy,
never ceasing,
Call for songs of
loudest praise.

Today's verse

DATE

quick notes _____
_____
_____
_____
_____

prayer items

Today's verse

DATE

quick notes

_____

_____

_____

_____

_____

prayer items

Today's verse

DATE

 quick notes

_____

_____

_____

_____

_____

prayer items

Today's verse

DATE

quick notes

_____
_____
_____
_____
_____

prayer items

Today's verse

DATE

quick notes

_____

_____

_____

_____

_____

prayer items

Do unto OTHERS as you would HAVE THEM do unto you

LUKE 6:31

Today's verse

DATE

quick notes

_____

_____

_____

_____

_____

prayer items

The LORD is my shepherd, I shall not want.

PSALM 23:1

Today's verse

DATE

quick notes

_____
_____
_____
_____
_____

prayer items

Today's verse

DATE

quick notes

_____
_____
_____
_____
_____

prayer items

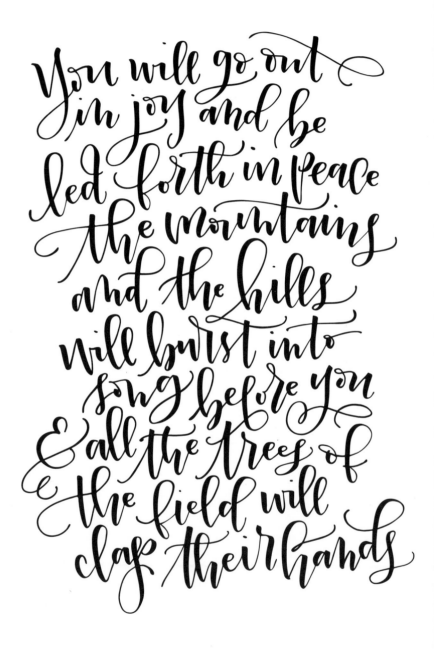

You will go out in joy and be led forth in peace the mountains and the hills will burst into song before you & all the trees of the field will clap their hands

Today's verse

DATE

quick notes
_____
_____
_____
_____
_____

prayer items

FOR No Word FROM GOD WILL EVER fail
-LUKE 1:36

Today's verse

DATE

quick notes

_____

_____

_____

_____

_____

prayer items

SEE WHAT *great love* THE FATHER HAS *lavished* ON US.

1 JOHN 3:1

Today's verse

DATE

quick notes

_____
_____
_____
_____
_____

prayer items

TASTE and see that the LORD is GOOD; BLESSED is the one who takes REFUGE in HIM.

PSALM 34·8

Today's verse

DATE

quick notes

_____

_____

_____

_____

_____

prayer items

DEUTERONOMY 31:6

Today's verse

DATE

quick notes
_____
_____
_____
_____
_____

prayer items

Today's verse

DATE

quick notes

_____

_____

_____

_____

_____

prayer items

Today's verse

DATE

quick notes

_____
_____
_____
_____
_____

prayer items

peace

Today's verse

DATE

quick notes

_____

_____

_____

_____

_____

prayer items

God, may your blessing be on my family

2 SAMUEL 7:29

Today's verse

DATE

quick notes

_____

_____

_____

_____

_____

prayer items

Search Me, O God & know my heart. Test me and know my anxious thoughts.

Today's verse

DATE

quick notes

_____
_____
_____
_____
_____

prayer items

And from his fullness we have all received grace upon grace.

JOHN 1:16

Today's verse

DATE

quick notes

_____

_____

_____

_____

_____

prayer items

Today's verse

DATE

quick notes _____

_____

_____

_____

_____

prayer items

As for me
and my house
we will serve
the Lord.

this is the
day
that the Lord
has made